To Eileen
with very best wishes
Peter Bland 2014

The Night Kite

for
George, Isabel & Alfred

The Night Kite

poems for children

Peter Bland

illustrated by
Carl Bland

MALLINSON RENDEL

The Night Kite

I flew our house
The other night.
It makes a lovely
Bright box-kite.

Like a big square moon
It slowly rose
Tied to a reel
Of garden hose.

As for the tail . . .
I'd had the sense
To borrow a length
Of our front fence.

It floated all night
Above our back lawn
While my sister sneezed
And my brother snored.

What shall I tell them
When they awake
About hoses that float
And houses in space?

I'll tell them nothing.
It wouldn't make sense.
I'll just reel in that hose
And sit on the fence.

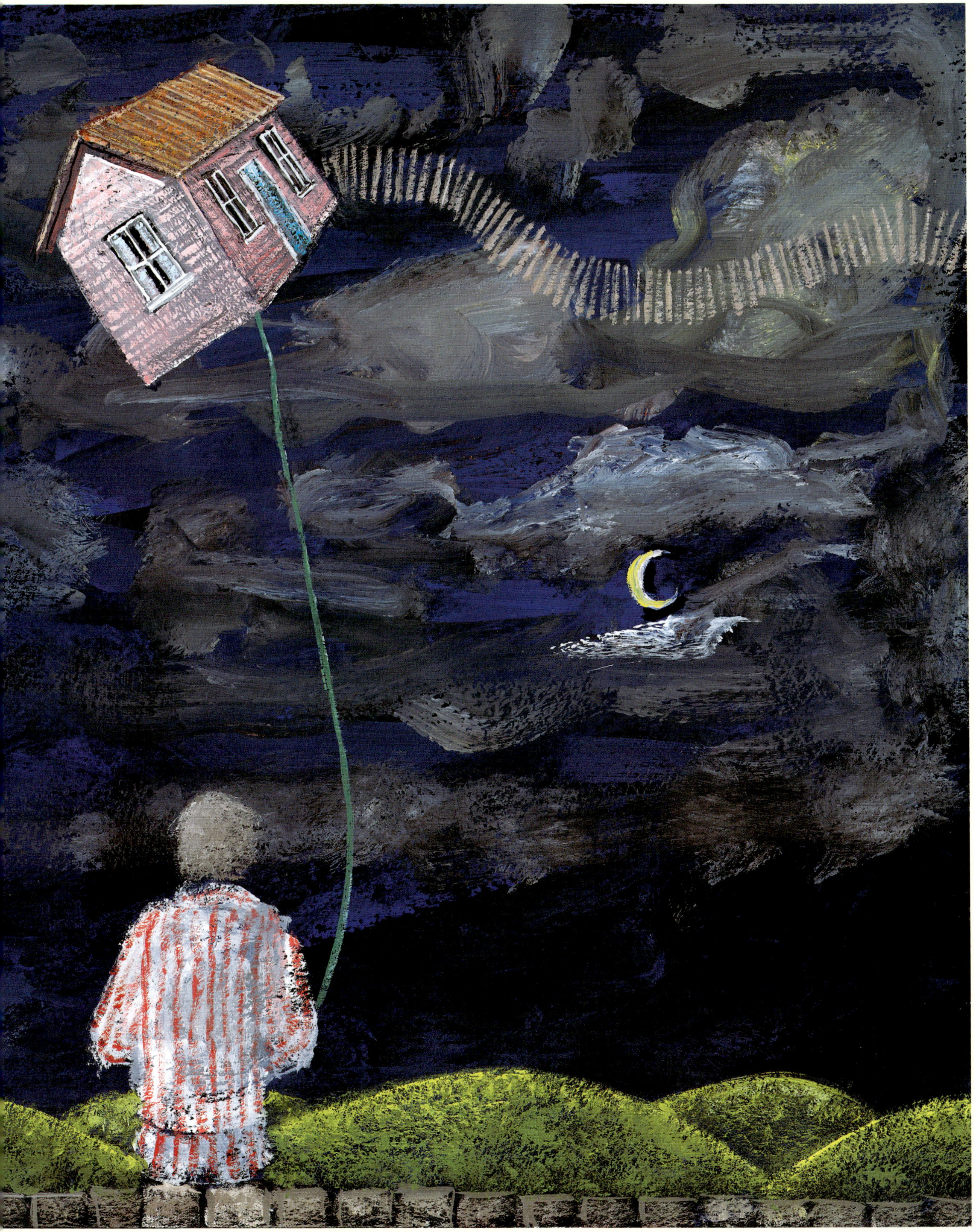

The Garden God

We've carved a garden god out of a log
and planted him in our cabbage patch.

He's painted blue. Whenever it rains
he weeps blue tears . . . but his curved

mouth laughs. We talk to him,
tell him which plants are in leaf;

we describe the colours of passing moths.
He beams and weeps. His weathered head

is full of little red ants.
Bees and butterflies bask on his chest.

We like to think of him as one of us.

Our Dog Charlie

Our dog Charlie
is such a softie that
sparrows eat their
breakfast
perched upon his
back.

No one's scared of
Charlie.
He smiles when
he's asleep
dreaming of days in
the country
being rounded up
by sheep.

The Little Blue Man

There's a little blue man
Like a piece of sky
Who walks round our house
Selling hot sun pies.

They're runny with honey
He stole from the bees
And shiny bee-stings
Stick out of his knees.

He sells them as needles
To little blue wives
Who live in the clouds
Baking more sun pies.

The Snail Party

The snails are having a party
behind our garden shed,
drinking rain from a jam-jar,
eating bits of stale bread.

They're piling up like pebbles
but they've left a silver path
back to where they came from
under the old bird-bath.

And now they're
having a party,
now they're having fun,
dragging their homes
behind them,
crawling before
they can
run.

Freddy the Fearless Caterpillar

Freddy's a fearless caterpillar.
He'll never ever run
And if you try to pick him up
He'll bite you on the thumb.

He'll never curl into a ball
Or hide behind a leaf.
He'll fell a four-foot hollyhock
With one snap of his teeth.

He'll never be a butterfly.
He'll never get his wings.
For Freddy is an earthy beast.
He bites and claws and stings.

His forty feet have little hooves.
He's a bull among the thorns.
He charges butterflies and moths
And belts them with his horns.

Eat It All Up

Roast lamb and potatoes
figs fresh from the tree
pipi and mussels
plum jam and tea

Gold hokey-pokey ice
-cream in a cone
baked beans and salmon
and ham off the bone

Pumpkin and kumara
peaches and plums
onions and gravy
and hot hot-cross buns

Mushrooms and strawberries
cheese on a stick
spaghetti and saveloys . . .
I think I'd be sick!

The Stone Owl

*for Jo
who
found
an owl
in
a stone*

The stone owl waited
on the edge of the stream:
ten million years
he slept his owl dream.

He waited through water
and fire and snow
for the seasons to shape
the owl in his soul.

Then the small child came
to play in the stream
and reached for the stone
to throw . . . but his feel

warmed the stone owl awake
and the small child cried
*There's an owl in this stone
He's alive! He's alive!*

Now the stone owl stands
looking out at the moon
from the high attic window
of the small child's room.

He has worn-away eyes
and a chipped-away beak
and heavy humped wings
and sharp flinty feet.

And he flies in his dreams
beyond any known bird
to a time long ago
when stones ruled the world.

He flies over oceans
that have dried up and gone,
over deserts where whales
once played in the sun.

He flies till he drops . . .
one more stone by a lake,
waiting for someone
to wish him awake.

Owl

Night owl
    White owl
Cold stars
    Moon red

Attic light
    Fire bright
Earth sleep
    Warm bed

Rhymes

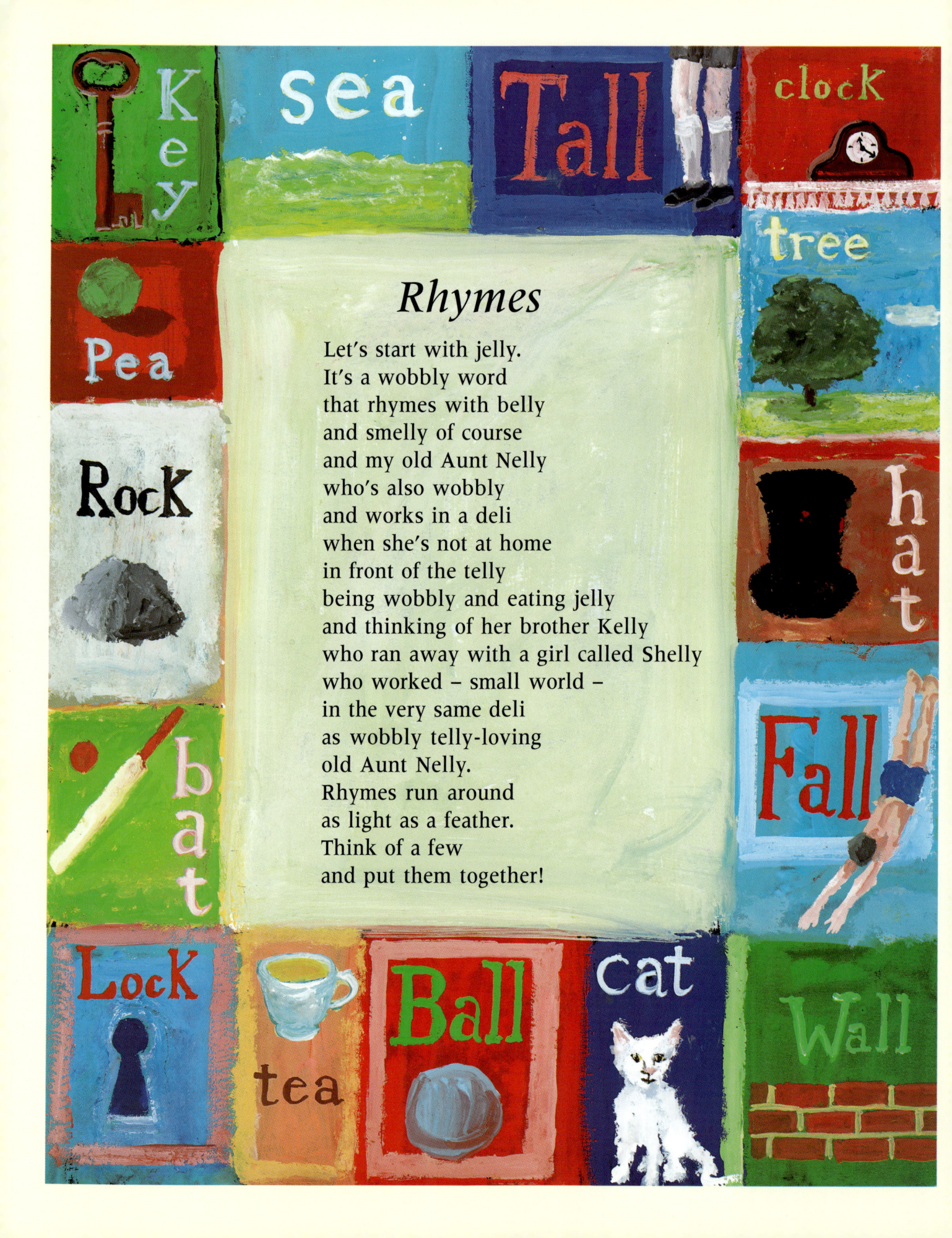

Let's start with jelly.
It's a wobbly word
that rhymes with belly
and smelly of course
and my old Aunt Nelly
who's also wobbly
and works in a deli
when she's not at home
in front of the telly
being wobbly and eating jelly
and thinking of her brother Kelly
who ran away with a girl called Shelly
who worked – small world –
in the very same deli
as wobbly telly-loving
old Aunt Nelly.
Rhymes run around
as light as a feather.
Think of a few
and put them together!

Glad

I'm glad
          I'm sad
I'm bad
          I'm mad
I'm gladsadbadmad
AND DON'T YOU
FORGET IT!

Mushrooming

Shhh! It's early.
We're being stealthy.
There's a mist on the ground
and no one's up.

We're like pirates
searching for buried treasure . . .
fat white doubloons
that gleam in the grass.

Eel Poem

I love

mud   drains

darkness

　　　　drowned sheep

I hate

sunlight

　　　bright water

eels   bigger   than   me

The Sugar Boat

Here comes the sugar boat
steaming in
from somewhere sunny
where dolphins swim.

It's full of sugar-cane
sweet and yummy.
Its funnel's yellow
and glows like honey.

It's followed by parrots
instead of gulls
and bees and butterflies
cling to its hull.

Humming-birds hum
and sunflowers flower
as it sails into town
like the first day of summer.

In Summer . . .

the tips of things
— grass, petals, twigs —
quiver with a ceaseless
insect shimmering

everywhere
there's the murmur of wings
a moth-blur
a gauzy quickening . . .

the entire landscape
is trying to take off!

Mozzie

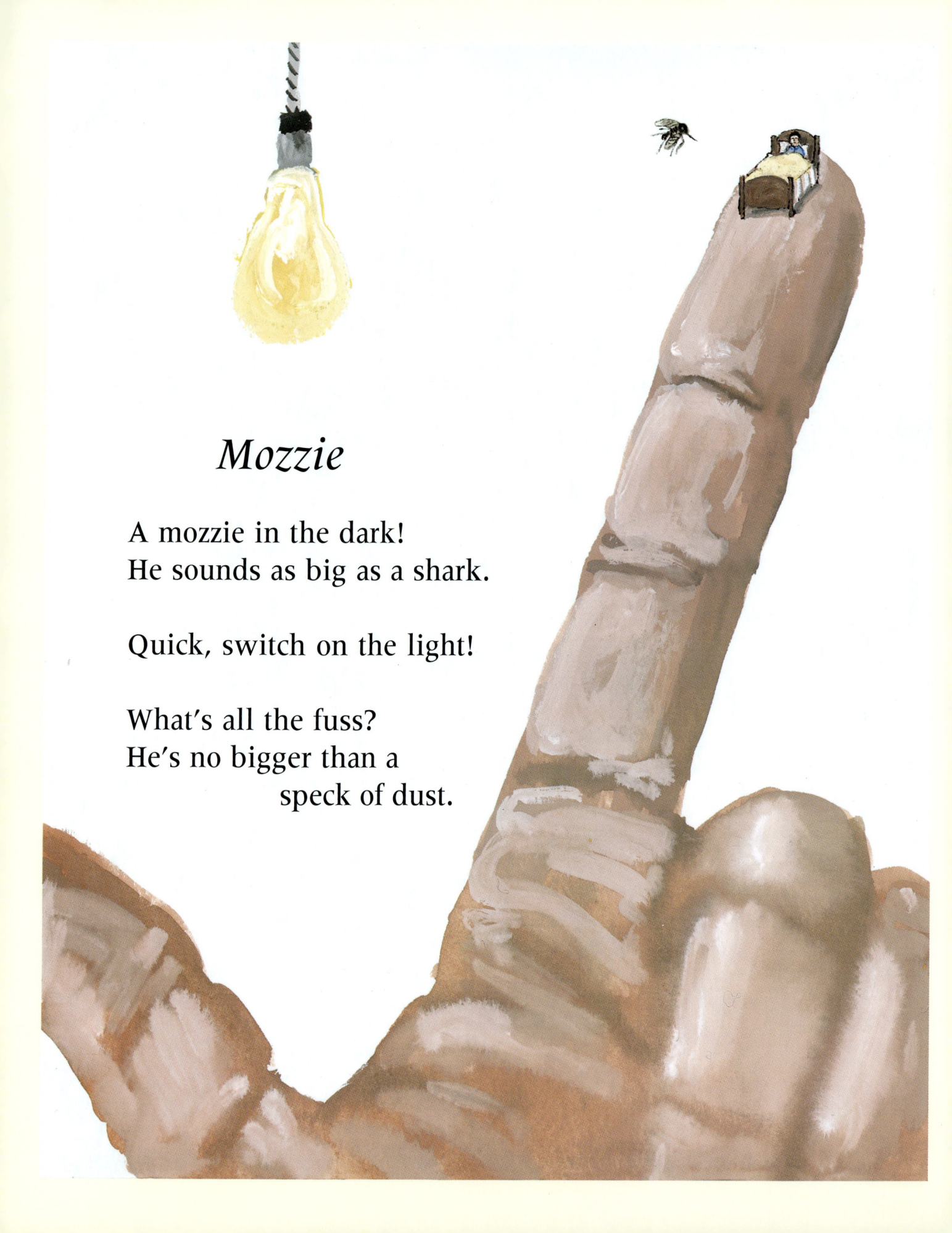

A mozzie in the dark!
He sounds as big as a shark.

Quick, switch on the light!

What's all the fuss?
He's no bigger than a
       speck of dust.

Kids Love Cats

Kids love cats
not cats that slash

but cats you can cuddle
that curl up in a bundle

and purrrrrrrrrrrr
when they're scratched.

Whales

Whales are as big as hills.
They're mostly black or grey.
If you ever see one coming
It's best to get out of the way.

The Moon Man

Down in the black bay
after dark
the moon man rides
on a silver shark.

Across the cold waves
he glides with no sound
as conger eels freeze
with tails pointing down.

Yes, conger eels freeze
floating stiff with fright
and jelly-fish pop
like powdered ice.

Is he evil or good?
No one can tell
but even rock oysters
stay in their shells.

While deep in their caves
the hermit-crabs pray
for a warm wind to blow
the moon man away.

Getting Ready to Go

I *think* we're getting ready to go.
Mum's packing bags. Dad's polishing the car.
Even Aunt Alice is cleaning her specs
and staring out at the road.

Perhaps there's a wedding or someone's sick
or we're spending *another* day at the zoo?
Or maybe Dad wants to buy a boat?
He's always talking of taking off
for places he's only read about.

Perhaps it's just that everyone's bored?
There's lots of talk about where to stay.
I suppose they'll decide *that* on the way
so that the journey is what it's about
and getting *anywhere* will be a surprise.

In the end I bet they'll change their minds
and watch TV or mow the lawn.
That's mostly what Mums and Dads seem to do
on a dull day with the threat of rain
and no particular place to go.

The Bed Boat

My bed is a boat.
The mattress won't leak.
My head-board's a rudder,
my sail is a sheet.

I sail every night
exploring my room,
past wardrobes like ships,
past mirrors like moons.

As I drift into sleep
my bed-boat sails on,
though where it sails to
is known to no one.

But when I wake up,
my voyage safely done,
I throw back the curtains
and let in the sun.

I Watch the Little Fishes

I watch the little fishes
nibble at my toes
and small green waves come marching in
like soldiers in smart rows.

I watch the hungry herons
walking round on stilts
and cormorants on the boat-shed
hanging out their wings.

I sometimes spot a sting-ray.
I sometimes spot a shark.
But I keep away from Bottomless Bay
and never stay after dark.

It's Time . . .

It's time to lock up the house.
It's time to head for the coast.
It's time to fill up the chilly-bin
And mess about in boats.

It's time to bag some mussels.
It's time to explore the beach.
It's time to tip-toe along the sands
Without ever burning your feet.

It's time to stare at the stars
And search for the man-in-the-moon.
It's time to swim and climb and run
And never go back to school.

Bear – Begging

A heap of blubber in a brown hair-shirt. He
hoists himself up and that hair-shirt rolls

down to his ankles. He's earthed in fat.
He's fast. He can catch like a bird. He

mouths from thin air the nuts and buns
we throw across a deep crevasse. We

hurl a sudden flurry of bread. He's not
put off. He knows just how far he can stretch.

He leans across the lip of his world
and swallows only the choicest bits.

White Cat, Black Cat

White cat, black cat,
Day or night cats,
I'd rather have striped cats
Than cats like these.

Coal cat, snow cat,
Hot or cold cats,
The skinniest two cats
I've ever seen.

Black-birds, white-mice,
Don't look round twice,
These cats aren't nice . . .
RUN FOR YOUR LIVES!

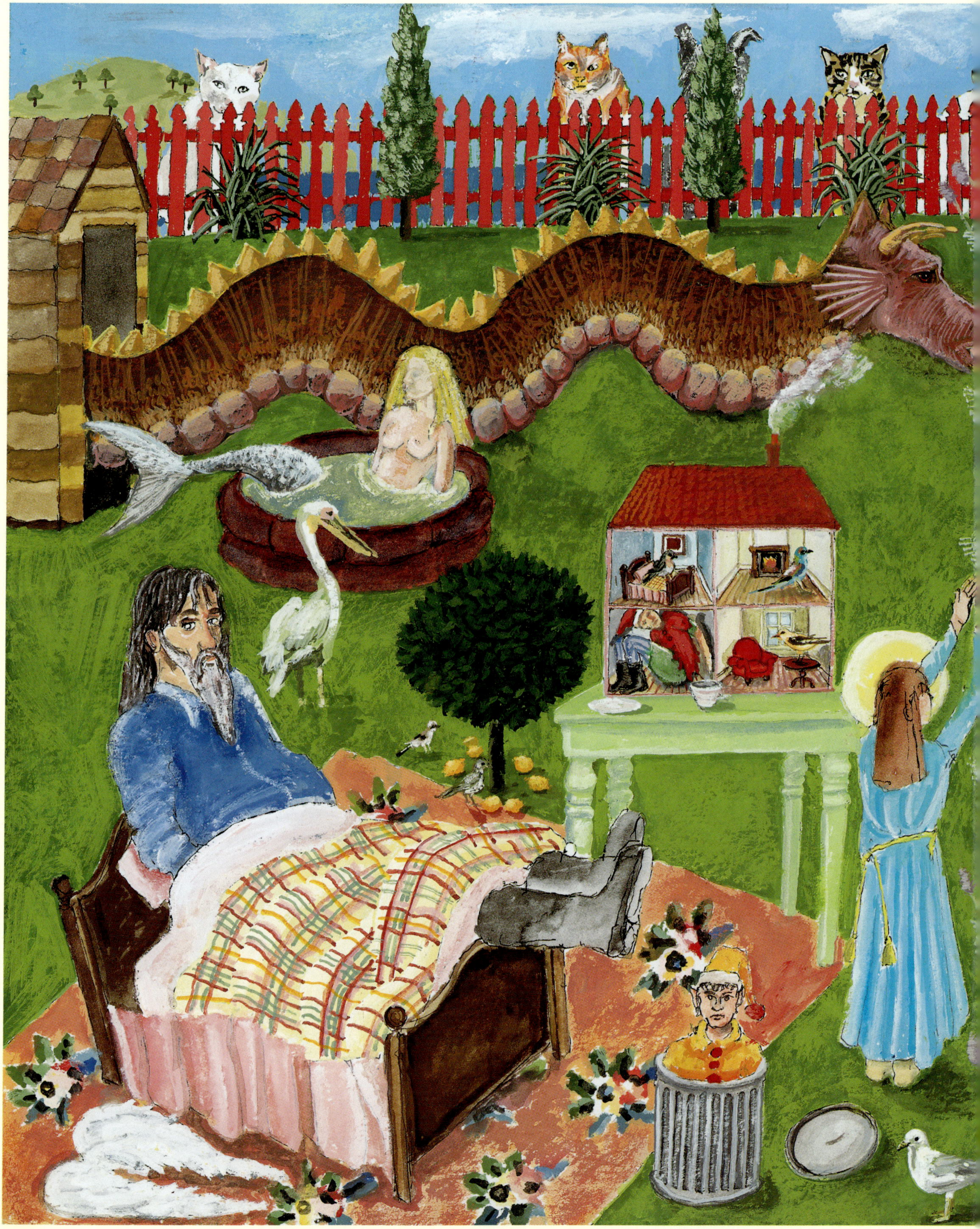

There's a Unicorn in the Garden

There's a unicorn in the garden
There's a dragon in Dad's shed
There's a mermaid in the paddling pool
There's a giant in my bed

There's a pixie in the doll's house
There's an angel who's lost her wings
There's a homeless gnome
          who's starting to moan
trapped in the rubbish bin

What are they doing in our street?
Why have they come to town?
Aren't they afraid that cats and dogs
will howl and hunt them down?

Perhaps they've come to say farewell?
Perhaps they're the last of their kind?
Perhaps there's nowhere left in the world
where imaginary things can hide?

PETER BLAND was born in Scarborough,
Yorkshire and emigrated to New Zealand at the age of twenty.
He studied English at Victoria University of Wellington and worked for a number
of years for the New Zealand Broadcasting Corporation, creating some of
New Zealand's first arts and social comment programmes.
In 1964 he became a free-lance writer/actor and a co-founder of Wellington's
Downstage Theatre. He has worked all over the world as an actor, appearing with
such well-known names as Bob Hope, Dave Allen, Victoria Wood, and Les Dawson.
He is perhaps best known in New Zealand for his role as Wesley Pennington
in the film *Came a Hot Friday*, for which he won a GOFTA Best Film Actor Award.

Peter began writing poetry shortly after arriving in New Zealand.
He found poetry invaluable as a way of exploring and understanding
a new country and his place in it. He has published eleven volumes of poetry and
is represented in every major New Zealand poetry anthology and several in the UK.
He has won numerous international awards for his work.
Peter lives in Auckland with his wife Beryl, to whom he has been
married for forty-nine years.

CARL BLAND, Peter's son, was born
in Lower Hutt but grew up in both New Zealand and the UK.
He obtained a BA with Honours at the Chelsea School of Art and has
had exhibitions of his work in Auckland and overseas.
Like his father, Carl is also a professional actor, well-known in
New Zealand for his stage, TV, and film appearances.

First published in 2004 by
Mallinson Rendel Publishers Ltd
P O Box 9409, Wellington
Text © Peter Bland, 2004
Illustrations © Carl Bland, 2004

Reprinted 2005

National Library of New Zealand
Cataloguing-in-Publication Data

Bland, Peter, 1934-
The night kite / by Peter Bland; illustrated by Carl Bland
ISBN 0-908783-83-3
1. Children's poetry, New Zealand. I. Bland, Carl. II. Title.
NZ821.1—dc21

Printed in China through Colorcraft Ltd., Hong Kong